The Homes of the Hoovers

by Ruth Dennis

Illustrations by William J. Wagner

Edited by Tom Walsh

Book design by Dick Blazek

CONTENTS

- Preface 1
1. An overview 2
2. Herbert Hoover's early homes 5
3. Herbert Hoover on his own 11
4. Lou Henry's early homes 20
5. Overseas addresses 25
6. The Lou Henry Hoover House 32
7. The Washington years 38
8. 1600 Pennsylvania Avenue 41
9. An oasis in the mountains 47
10. High above Manhattan 52
- Appendix 58

WHERE HERBERT HOOVER WAS BORN, SERVED AND DIED

PREFACE

Having had parents and a husband who were Hoover boosters, it was only natural that, in time, I applied for the position of librarian of the book collection at the newly built Herbert Hoover Presidential Library at West Branch. With a great deal of help from my fellow workers, the library was ready for researchers on schedule, and my study of the Hoovers started.

After my retirement, I continued to do research there for scholars and authors and, with encouragement from Dr. Joan Hoff Wilson and Dr. Susan Kennedy, historians and authors about Hoover, I started researching for myself. Mildred Mather, who took my position as librarian, but was in truth more of an archivist, prodded me continually, with help all the way, to write about both Lou Henry and Herbert Hoover.

Through the research that has enriched my life and studying, especially the Oral Histories, I became aware of the need of documenting the humanness and humor of our former President and his wife. This book is part of what I have to say about the greatness of this couple. It is not my intent to write about every place Hoover spent a night, fortnight or even a few months.

I owe special thanks and appreciation to those already mentioned and to many others. Bill Wagner, who agreed to illustrate some of the homes, has encouraged me on countless occasions. John Fawcett, executive director of the Hoover Presidential Library Association, has been most helpful, feeling the need for this book. Dr. George Nash, whose definitive biography of Herbert Hoover is giving the scholarly version of his life and works, has been most helpful and enthusiastic in his support of my effort. Tom Walsh, my editor, has "kept me at it" with his encouragement, advice in punctuation, syntax and organization of my material and his abounding enthusiasm. And my family, who have given me loving and practical help in my project.

I am grateful beyond words to all, as well as to the dear friends who bore with me in my enthusiasm for trying to focus in on the humanness of two great Americans, Lou Henry and Herbert Hoover.

—*Ruth Dennis*

CHAPTER ONE:
An overview

Lou Henry no doubt had an inkling of what a whirlwind life as Mrs. Herbert Hoover would be like, but that was no deterrent to an affirmative response to mining engineer Herbert Hoover's cablegram marriage proposal from the outback of Australia.

After nearly two years of working in the gold fields of Western Australia, Herbert Hoover and Lou Henry were married in California in 1899 and were immediately off to China. There the newlyweds would see the bloody Boxer Rebellion transform their home into a besieged fortress. The Hoovers' world travels eventually would bring them three addresses in and around London, seven different addresses in California, one in New York City, one in Virginia and five in Washington, D.C.—including the most famous address of all: 1600 Pennsylvania Avenue.

After Lou Henry's death in 1944, the ex-president had just one address of his own: Suite 31-A of New York's Waldorf-Astoria Towers, where he died in 1964.

Over the global course of the Hoovers' 44-year marriage, many friends commented on Lou Henry Hoover's ability to establish a home under virtually any circumstances. After Lou Henry Hoover's death, longtime friend Ray Lyman Wilbur expressed it best: "Wherever she went, she made a home for her husband and her children. She had a great skill in making domestic things simple, in welcoming and entertaining guests, and in providing a background of comfort for the household, particularly for her husband. His friends and associates became at once her friends and associates."

Ray Lyman Wilbur was among those who felt Lou Henry had much to do with making Hoover what he was, including a man who treasured his home. "Lou Henry Hoover could deal as understandingly and sympathetically with a gardener as with the head of a world conference," he said. "Her mind was scientific, her training good, her mental discipline excellent. She was capable of sustained work, and needed to be so in order to keep up with her family job. These qualities were invaluable to her husband."

Born in 1874 into the austerity of his Quaker family's two-room West Branch home, Herbert Hoover remarked in 1919 that he and Lou Henry were pursuing an American dream by planning a new home at Stanford University in California. "We all think we can build a better house than anybody ever built before, and every American family is entitled to this experience once in a lifetime," he said.

Lou Henry Hoover's involvement in the homes she shared with her husband and their children was a hands-on affair. Not only did she manage those households, she had a hand in designing more than one. She and Herbert chose the site for their California dream home, a hilltop where, as Stanford University students, they once courted. She was fond of fireplaces. She saw to it that the house they built on that hilltop had a fireplace in every principal room and another outside for toasting marshmallows and weiners. Lou Henry kept her pewter collection in the dining room of their Stanford house hidden behind secret panels in its walls. It was an arrangement she devised not out of fear of theft, but out of disdain for hinges and knobs.

When the Hoovers oversaw the construction of a presidential retreat in the Blue Ridge Mountains west of Washington D.C., it was clear who was in charge at Camp Rapidan.. At least it was clear to Marine Corps

The Huber house in Oberkulm, Switzerland, where Johan Heinrich Huber — the great great great great great grandfather of Herbert Clark Hoover was born in 1644.

Captain W.W. Rogers, who was assigned to work on the project. "Of course she was sort of opinionated," he said of Lou Henry. "She wanted things like she wanted them, and that's what we were there for—to do things like they wanted them, so we tried the best we could."

The architectural insight Lou Henry Hoover brought to her own homes she also shared. When a couple who worked for the Hoovers in the White House—Katurah and Phillips Brooks—were considering building a house, Lou Henry was quick to offer her advice. "Katurah," she said, "if you ever decide to build a house, be sure to have your kitchen on the southern exposure. You get the sun all day. It comes up and it comes over and you get it in your kitchen all day." The couple took her advice and were delighted.

Lou Henry shared her insights into fireplaces, too. In 1939, the Hoovers were the dinner guests of Thomas Dewey, a lawyer who would later be elected governor of New York and make an unsuccessful bid for the presidency. During the dinner in the Dewey home in New York City, the fireplace began to smoke. There was a moment of panic until Lou Henry Hoover got up from the table and casually adjusted the damper to stop the outpour of smoke.

The homes of the Hoovers—those that remain and others long gone—are reflections of the busy lives they sheltered. From Lou Henry's secret study at Stanford to the ever-present scratching stones the pipe-smoking ex-president kept around his Waldorf suite for striking kitchen matches, the homes of the Hoovers shed new and particularly human light on the private lives of public people.

CHAPTER TWO:
Herbert Hoover's early homes

About a year after his March 12, 1870, marriage to Hulda Minthorn, a young blacksmith named Jesse C. Hoover paid $90 for two lots in West Branch, Iowa, with the idea of providing a home for his family. The couple's first child, Theodore ("Tad"), had been born the last week of January, 1871.

Assisted by his father, Eli, Jesse built a two-room, board and batten cottage on one of the two lots. Boulders used for foundation stones were hauled by wagon from the open prairie to the west. Auger holes, still visible in the rafters, show the timbers from which the framework of the cottage were hewn had been lashed together and rafted down the Mississippi River from Wisconsin or Minnesota to a Muscatine sawmill. There they were cut into lumber and hauled by oxcart overland to West Branch, 30 miles away.

When completed, the cottage faced east on Downey Street and measured 14-by-20 feet. The front door, which was fashioned with a thumb latch, opened into a room that served as a parlor, kitchen and dining area. On the south end of the cottage was its only bedroom, not quite 14-by-7 feet. On August 10, 1874, in that tiny bedroom, Herbert Hoover was born. At the rear of the cottage was a wood shed to the north. It had various uses, one being sleeping quarters for men hired to assist Jesse in his blacksmith shop. A hired man named E.D. Smith was asleep there on the night Herbert Hoover was born and was awakened and sent to summon assistance.

After the birth of Mary ("May") in 1876, it became obvious the Hoover family needed a larger home; the two boys were sleeping in a trundle bed with their parents, while May slept in a little cradle of her own. In May of 1878, the same year Jesse Hoover went into the farm implement business, he sold his family's tiny cottage, his blacksmith shop and the adjoining property for $1,000.

Birthplace becomes a kitchen

Herbert Hoover's birthplace cottage was eventually resold in 1890 to R.P. Scellars, a carpenter. After buying another house and moving it onto the lot, Mr. Scellars turned the birthplace cottage 90 degrees so that it faced south, instead of east. Once the two buildings were joined, Herbert Hoover's birthplace became a kitchen for the larger house depicted in Grant Wood's 1931 oil painting entitled "The Birthplace of Herbert Hoover."

It was in 1927 that Lou Henry Hoover first attempted to buy her husband's birthplace and restore it to its original condition. But Mrs. Scellars, who assumed ownership of the cottage after her husband's death in 1916, did not want to sell it, at any price. By charging 10-cents admission and selling hot dogs, postcards and a few souvenirs, she was making about $600 a year. Since she was taking good care of the property and was not tempted to sell by additional offers of more money, she retained ownership until her death in 1934. Her heirs decided in 1935 to sell the cottage. Since Herbert Hoover knew his wife and sons were anxious to buy the birthplace, he asked a friend, Fred Albin, to buy it. This he did, paying $4,500, and he immediately sold it to Hoover's son, Allan.

BIRTHPLACE OF HERBERT HOOVER, WEST BRANCH, IOWA

With the cottage once again in the hands of the Hoover family, the effort to restore it to its original condition began. The Hoover family financed the project and bought additional land around the cottage. On December 1, 1939, a deed was recorded that transferred title to the birthplace cottage, a newly built caretaker's house and the land surrounding them from Allan Hoover to the Herbert Hoover Birthplace Society. That group, organized April 1, 1939, merged in 1958 with the Herbert Hoover Birthplace Foundation. In 1973, the organization became the modern-day Herbert Hoover Presidential Library Association. Once restored to its original form, the birthplace cottage became the centerpiece of the present-day Herbert Hoover National Historic Site.

"Second house" has more room

It's unclear where the Hoover family lived for the year following the sale of the birthplace cottage in 1878. A deed shows that on March 20, 1879, Jesse Hoover bought what has been described as a "commodious" four-room, two-story home a block south and across Downey Street from Herbert Hoover's birthplace cottage. An item in The West Branch Local Record of May 29, 1879, reads, "Mr. J.C. Hoover moved into his new house Tuesday morning and is now 'as snug as a bug in a rug.'" The white house known as the Hoovers' "second house" was surrounded by trees—maple trees lined the front yard, and a wild crabapple tree grew out back. There was a barn on the southeast corner of the lot and a garden with potato vines and grape arbors. It was this house and one-acre lot where Herbert Hoover spent much of the next five years and which he associated with his boyhood memories.

By all accounts, Herbert—"Bertie"—and his brother Tad were active boys who roamed the woods, played in the Wapsinonoc Creek that ran between their boyhood homes and, in winter, coasted down nearby Cook's hill. All in all, their activities were normal for boys of that time and place. But sadness would soon color the lives of the Hoover children. On December 13, 1880, Jesse Hoover died at age 34. In spite of protests from the family, Hulda Hoover insisted on singing Jesse's favorite song at his funeral, "From Greenland's Icy Mountains."

Keeping the family together

After Jesse Hoover's death, Hulda was determined to keep her family together. She was helped by various relatives, who assisted her financially in any way they could. One summer she took the children to northwest Iowa to visit with relatives. While there, they lived with an uncle, Pennington Minthorn, in his sod house in Sioux County. Another summer, Bertie traveled by train and buggie to Pawhuska, Indian Territory (now Oklahoma), where he spent several months living with his mother's sister, Agnes, and her husband, Laban J. Miles. A relative of General Nelson A. Miles, a famous American Indian fighter, Laban Miles was the government agent to the Osage and Kaw Indian nations.

"They had a boy and girl about my age, and Aunt Agnes was a kindly person and a good cook,"

HERBERT HOOVER'S SECOND HOME, WEST BRANCH, IOWA.

OSAGE AGENCY HOUSE   PAWHUSKA, OKLAHOMA

Herbert Hoover recalled in 1958. "They lived in a great stone house with big fireplaces."

Today, the Pawhuska house is a lovely old mansion at 621 Granview Street. The windows are recessed into walls nearly nine inches thick. Originally built in the style of an English country house, it has been remodeled over the years to the tastes of a variety of occupants. When Hoover stayed there, the entryway was at the center of the front wall, with a stairway leading to the second floor from the front door. Today, there is a widow's walk at the top of the house. The lovely shade trees that surround it were mere saplings in the 1880s.

Herbert Hoover and his two cousins attended Sunday school in Pawhuska with Indian children, who practiced their English on the three of them. "At Sunday School one time," he later recalled, "the lesson was on Annanias and Sephira. When the Indian children were asked the title of the lesson—to the joy of us three—the little Indians piped up, 'Annanias set fire-a to his wife.'"

Tragedy strikes again

Tragedy struck again on February 24, 1884, when Hulda Hoover died in West Branch at age 35 of typhoid fever and pneumonia. Lawrie Tatum, a pioneer farmer and well-known Quaker, was appointed guardian of the orphaned Hoover children, while various relatives offered to care for them.

Today, nothing remains of the two-story home these newly orphaned children left behind except photographs and memories. It was sold for $500 in April 1886 and torn down in the fall of 1923. In 1971, it was suggested that the house be reconstructed, but that recommendation has not been pursued.

CHAPTER THREE:
Herbert Hoover on his own

After his mother's death in 1884, Herbert Hoover, not yet 10 years old, continued to live near West Branch with his Uncle Allen and Aunt Millie Hoover on their farm about one mile north of the West Branch depot. In the fall of 1885, his mother's brother, Dr. Henry John Minthorn, and his wife, Laura, invited Bertie to live with them and their two daughters in Newberg, Oregon. The Minthorns had recently lost a son, and it was thought that Herbert would help ease their grief. His relatives also felt that there would be educational advantages, since Dr. Minthorn had recently become superintendent of a Quaker academy in Newberg.

"Oregon was a new world to be explored," Herbert Hoover recalled 73 years later. "It was here I first met with fish and unlimited fruit, which grew right in the back yard."

The Minthorns lived in a white, two-story wooden frame house which had been built a few years earlier. The house had a big cellar, which Herbert Hoover later referred to as Aunt Laura's "own social security."

"She and Uncle John stowed vegetables and apples and pears," he recalled. "Also, under discipline, we three youngsters had to prepare for Christmas by making unlimited jars of jam, jelly and especially pear butter as there were three pear trees.

"That pear butter became a great trial to me. Aunt Laura made it in a kettle over an outdoor fire, and I had to stir it for what seemed hours. Aunt Laura, however, was a generous soul and told me to eat all the pears I liked. I like pears, but after a time Aunt Laura had to put me to bed with a dose of peppermint oil. I did not eat a pear again, even at Christmas, for years."

Off to Stanford

In 1888, the Minthorns and Herbert Hoover moved to Salem, Orgeon, living temporarily in a barn until moving into a new home at Hazel and Highland avenues. Herbert Hoover quit school to go to work for the Oregon Land Company, a job he held for three years, from 1888 to 1891. On August 29, 1891, less than three weeks after his 17th birthday, Herbert Hoover boarded a train in Salem for the newly formed Stanford University in California. After some tutoring in geometry and some additional entrance examinations, he was accepted. He had come to Stanford with a friend from Salem, Fred Williams, and together they became the first Stanford students to be assigned to Encina Hall, a men's dormitory. It was the beginning of many "firsts" for Hoover while at Stanford, including being a member of the university's first graduating class.

Although he was reported to be the first student to sleep in Encina Hall, Herbert Hoover soon felt he could not afford the $15 a month, plus board, it was costing him to live there. Consequently, according to one story, he and others in similar financial straits moved into the "Camp," a collection of barracks-like rooms erected for the workmen who built the new university. The rent was nominal, and they found it possible to "batch" it there and to reduce their living costs.

"The floors of the Camp rooms were about two feet from the ground; in some the boards were loose and would get slipped aside," wrote John F. Newsome, a mining engineer and author who attended Stanford at the same time as Mr. Hoover. "The Chinese cooks at the Camp, where a number of workmen

MINTHORN HOME   NEWBERG, OREGON

MINTHORN HOME   SALEM, OREGON

still roomed and boarded, always had a lot of chickens, and these chickens would wander under the floors as chickens are prone to do when it rains.

"It was rumored (and the Chinamen surely believed the rumor) that occasional chickens either wandered maliciously or were enticed by scattered grains of corn up through the loose boards of the floor and disappeared. I cannot vouch for the truth of this rumor; neither did I ever hear young Hoover's name mentioned in connection with these lost chicken episodes. Judging from the general situation, however, I would say that any chicken that either willfully or unwillingly went up into one of those rooms through a hole in the floor confronted a situation of extreme gravity."

If Herbert Hoover ever did live in the "Camp," it wasn't for long. During his second year at Stanford he returned to Romero Hall and spent his third and final years in Encina Hall.

During different summers, Herbert Hoover worked for two noted geologists, John Caspar Branner and Waldemar Lindgren. As his work took him to the Gold Belt and Grass Valley regions of California, into the Sierra Nevada Mountains in both California and Nevada, and into Arkansas and Oklahoma, the various places he stayed during those summers while studying and mapping could hardly be called homes.

After graduating from Stanford in May 1895 and eventually working underground for a few months in various gold mines near Nevada City, California, Herbert Hoover landed a job in 1896 in San Francisco with Louis Janin, an eminent mining engineer. His new job yielded happiness in the form of a home life with his brother, Tad, who was a linotype operator for the Oakland Tribune; his sister, May, who came from Oregon to attend school; and his cousin, Harriet, who lived with them in a house in Oakland while she attended Stanford. Although a few months later they would move together to Berkeley, the Hoover children, orphaned since 1884, were again reunited in Oakland.

An overseas address

It was through Louis Janin that Herbert Hoover was hired by Bewick, Moreing and Company of London to go to Western Australia for mine examination and exploration in the gold-mining interior near Coolgardie and Kalgoorlie—towns less than five years old.

He sailed for Australia from New York on March 31, 1897, with a short stopover in London at the company's office. He started work in the hot, arid outback at Coolgardie in May. Burlap bags and corrugated iron were used in building the first houses. Herbert Hoover's first home there was in the company-owned bungalow, with the services of a cook and valet.

"At one time I tried to enrich the living at our corrugated iron staff residence by growing a vegetable garden," he writes in his Memoirs. "It started well. But a large variety of creeping things, including several species of ants, entered into competition with each other. We managed to pull two cabbages through. Anyway the neighbors all collected on the fence every morning to watch a green thing grow."

Though headquartered at Coolgardie for nearly a year, Herbert Hoover was inspecting mines in the rugged outback, sometimes as far away as 300 miles. In 1897 alone, he traveled 210 miles by camel, 2,481 miles by team and 2,895 miles by train.

THE REUNION HOME   OAKLAND, CALIFORNIA

BEWICK, MOREING AND COMPANY BUNGALOW
KALGOORLIE, WESTERN AUSTRALIA

In a letter to Burt Brown Barker, Herbert Hoover advised his boyhood friend from Salem, Oregon, not to come to Western Australia. "It's a country of red dust, black flies and white heat," he wrote. "I could not portray the misery of any one of them on paper."

After Bewick, Moreing and Company obtained control of the Sons of Gwalia mine at Mt. Lenora, 150 miles north of Kalgoorlie, Herbert Hoover became its superintendent, a position he filled from May to November 1898. He and the miners pitched tents and lived in them until permission was granted to build more permanent buildings.

"Eventually, Gwalia had its own churches, schools (both state and convent), police station, fire brigade, post office, shops, Workers' Hall, sports oval and hotel," Don and Donna Reid said in their historical sketch book of Gwalia and Leonora. "For most of its life, its population was larger than that of Leonora.

"...Apart from one or two rooms built of stone, Gwalia was a town of timber and corrugated iron, with internal linings of whitewashed or painted hessians and filter cloth...Outside, whitewash or kalsomine was the main finish to the iron, giving a predominantly white aspect to the town.

"Gardens were cultivated around most houses and huts, even if it meant a grapevine or two and a small vegetable plot. The back yards contained chicken pens and pigeon lofts, usually constructed out of all sorts of odds and ends of wire netting, old iron and piping, secondhand timber and discarded water tanks.

"Inside, many of the houses and huts were full of improvised furniture and utensils...Wages were not high, life could be hard and no one spent money unnecessarily."

The Reids note that Herbert Hoover selected the site for the mine manager's house on the ridge north of the mine, at the eastern end of the row of staff houses. "It is typical of the expansive style of home built for the senior man on the mine during the period," they say in their sketchbook. "Its construction was begun by Hoover, though he was transferred to China before the building was completed in 1899."

The house is constructed of locally made brick, fired nearby, and bought under a contract which supplied bricks at 2 pounds, 10 shillings per thousand, plus supply of the fuel. A wide veranda once extended around three sides of the house. The timber throughout is imported Oregon pine.

The house was built with a lounge-dining room, and two bedrooms were soon extended to double their original size. The house is surrounded by gardens, which have been tended by a succession of Italian gardeners. Inside, a servant call system was installed in each room, to let the maid know where she was required. A full-time cook was accommodated in a back room, and a yardman was required to keep the kitchen supplied with wood and, in the winter, four fireplaces.

Herbert Hoover later visited the completed house in 1902 after becoming a partner in Bewick, Moreing and Company. But that was in the future. In the autumn of 1898, after a year-and-a-half "down under," he left Australia. His next assignment was to be technical adviser to the Chinese director-general of mines in two provinces in China. The Chinese saw the value of gold and silver mines and were anxious to develop them, but Charles Algernon Moreing of Bewick, Moreing and

Company knew that coal as well as precious metals was what China needed for future development.

During his stay in Australia, Mr. Hoover stayed in touch by letter and overseas cable with Lou Henry, a woman he had first met at Stanford. With his new assignment, Herbert Hoover's salary was increased, and he felt that, after a long separation, it was time to send a proposal of marriage by telegram to Lou. Her answer from California was affirmative.

SONS OF GWALIA MINE MANAGER'S HOME
MOUNT LENORA, WESTERN, AUSTRALIA

CHAPTER FOUR:
Lou Henry's Early Homes

Lou Henry was born March 29, 1874, in Waterloo, Iowa, about 60 miles from the West Branch birthplace of her future husband, Herbert Hoover, who was born later that same year on August 10.

It is said that her father, Charles D. Henry, was hoping for a son because he was an outdoorsman. Lou proved no disappointment to him, as she liked fishing, camping and riding—bareback and Western saddle, as well as the mandatory side-saddle. Her father discovered early in her life that Lou enjoyed hiking in the woods with him and learning from him the wonders of nature.

As a niece later wrote of Lou, "She was blue-eyed, bobbed hair, tanned; she was full of vitality."

Charles D. Henry and his wife, Florence, moved their family in 1876 from the Waterloo house where Lou was born to a farmhouse a mile west of Shell Rock, Iowa. Her father had an interest in a woolen mill there, and her mother helped out in the mill at times. Though only a small girl, Lou Henry was remembered by her Shell Rock contemporaries as a vivacious and adventurous youngster.

Leaving Iowa behind

The Henrys left Shell Rock in 1878, living briefly in Texas before returning to Waterloo. In 1884, when Lou was 10, the family again moved West, hoping that the move would improve Lou's mother's health. Enroute, they lived briefly in Clearwater, Kansas, before settling in the Quaker community of Whittier, California. A bookkeeper and a banker, Charles D. Henry established Whittier's first bank.

When Lou was 16, her father was asked to establish a bank in Monterey, California. After moving there, she and her father continued their hikes and nature studies together. She had a younger sister, Jean, who had great talent as a violinist. As hoped, her mother's health improved in California, and the Henrys had a happy family life there.

Lou decided to be a teacher, her mother's profession in Shell Rock, Iowa, before she was married. Lou specialized in biology and geology and graduated from San Jose Normal School, now San Jose State University. It was while at Normal that she met Dr. John Caspar Branner, a geologist who had come over from Stanford University to lecture. She became so interested in geology, she asked about studying the subject under Dr. Branner. It was at Stanford that she met Herbert Hoover.

A wedding in her family home

Upon graduating from Stanford in 1898, Lou Henry returned to Monterey to teach. After their lengthy separation, Herbert Hoover cabled Lou Henry his marriage proposal from the outback of Australia. Mr. and Mrs. Charles Henry sent out the announcement of their eldest daughter's marriage to Herbert Hoover in their home in Monterey on February 10, 1899, with an At Home address of Tientsin, China.

On March 12, 1899, Florence Henry, Lou's mother, wrote a letter to a friend about the 11 a.m. wedding ceremony. "Mr. Hoover and I stood in the bay window of the sitting room, as Charlie brought Lou through the little hall and gave her to the man that in a very short time was her husband. She wore a brown traveling suit, as did Mr. Hoover. They were

BIRTHPLACE OF LOU HENRY, WATERLOO, IOWA

LOU HENRY'S SECOND HOME, SHELL ROCK, IOWA

THE HOOVERS' WEDDING HOUSE, MONTEREY, CALIFORNIA

a perfect match. Neither knew what the other would wear as he bought his in New York or London, on his way here.

"Who he looks like is a question that I can not answer," she wrote. "He is five feet eleven inches and usually weighs one hundred and sixty pounds, and now has a smooth face. He had never been to the house but once. Had dinner with us before he went to Australia. We made up our minds not to like him very well as he was going to take Lou so far away, but after he had been here a few days (he stayed with us nine days before they were married, as Lou said she would not go until just before they sailed) I think we all like him about as much as Lou did. When his London firm wanted to know if he would go to China, from Australia, he said he would if they gave him time to go to the United States first. So he came all that distance—just to get Lou—had no other business whatever. As Lou is so fond of traveling and going among strangers, the proposed life seemed her ideal one."

CHAPTER FIVE:
Overseas Addresses

After almost a month aboard the steamship "Copic," with brief stops in Honolulu and Yokahama, Herbert Hoover and his bride, Lou Henry, arrived in Shanghai, China. It was March 20, 1899, when the newlyweds finally set foot in Tientsin, a city of 500,000 about 60 miles southeast of Peking.

Within two weeks of their arrival, Herbert Hoover started traveling to different gold mines in the provinces of Chihli and Jehol, inspecting, analyzing, appraising and evaluating prospects and mines. During that first journey, Lou Henry remained in Tientsin at the Astor House hotel and with friends. Later, the Hoovers moved into a rented, two-story, blue brick house on Racecourse Road, where they lived for nearly a year with the help of 15 Chinese servants who lived nearby.

"Mrs. Hoover had the excitements of trying to furnish it from Chinese availabilities and equipping it with the necessary multitude of Chinese servants," Herbert Hoover wrote later in the volume of his Memoirs subtitled Years of Adventure.

Since their rented home was at the edge of the foreign community, Lou Henry had the companionship of neighbors, as well as a number of Stanford friends who had moved to China. When she was left alone, which was much of the time, she helped her husband with articles he was writing for mining and geological periodicals. This undoubtedly aided him in the ability to have so many published.

When Lou Henry accompanied her husband on his mine inspection tours, they traveled on horseback, foregoing use of sedan chairs, to which Herbert Hoover's position entitled them. A geologist, too, Lou Henry would also go underground into the mines with him, an unprecedented act for a woman in China.

While in China, Lou Henry started collecting porcelain, semi-precious stones and artifacts. Over the years, these increased in value and brought the Hoovers joy in their own homes and as they shared them with friends. This was especially true of the "blue and whites," as the Chinese porcelain was known. It became an absorbing hobby for both of them that lasted all their lives.

For their day-to-day tableware, the Hoovers turned to the United States. A January 12, 1900, letter from Herbert Hoover to his sister-in-law, Jean, tells how he had asked his brother, Tad, and Tad's wife, Mildred, to ship them a set of dishes. The dishes arrived, but were a disappointment. Herbert Hoover told Jean that, despite describing "accurately with drawings what we wanted" and sending "long specifications of what we did not want," the dishes sent by Tad "were exactly what we did not want."

A typical day in China

In that same letter, Bert Hoover gaves Jean Henry this humorous account of their daily schedule in Tientsin:
"1. Get up 8:00 (ideal)
2. Have breakfast
3. Have Chinese Teacher, 8:30-10:30 for me and 10:30-11:30 Lou
4. I go to the office until 1:00. Lou rides her bike on uncertain errands.
5. Have tiffin at 1:00 (and swear at new dishes)

RACE COURSE ROAD HOME   TIENTSIN, CHINA

6. I go to office until 4:30. Lou works on various projects of ours chiefly statistics these days (ideal)
7. We go for horseback cart or bicycle ride until 6:30 or Lou receives callers.
8. Lou begins to dress at 6:30 for events that begin at 9:30 (Ideal!). I ponder our weighty problems, see her a moment when she comes down to snatch a bite of dinner. We usually arrive at the event at 10:00. (Lou has been reading thus far and is exceeding angry) Then I deliver her over to the innumerable admirers and go home or to the club or to have business consultations until 1:00 or 2:00 o'clock. Go and get her and go to bed. Sometimes we vary this by going out to dinner or somebody comes here. In this case she begins dressing at 4:30. Otherwise the same. Lou says this is neither humor nor wit but pure slander."

In the same mail was Lou's letter to her sister, which started out: "Have just been reading that idiotic boy's stupid letter. We are not half as bad as he would make you believe. It is true we don't have breakfast at 8:00 (except ideally) but you never expected I would. To get up early when not under compulsion of some form, is a thing one Henry would never believe of another! And only twice have I been late dressing to go places..."

As their schedule indicates, both Lou Henry and Herbert Hoover studied Chinese at home. Lou Henry learned to speak the language quite well, while Herbert Hoover claimed to have learned only 100 words or so. He said he held onto these so that, back in a crowd, he could say a few private words to Mrs. Hoover without others knowing what he was saying.

"She reads Chinese readily," Herbert Hoover wrote to his father-in-law, Charles Henry, "and constantly keeps me open to insult because any English speaking Chinaman in town always addresses her in Chinese and me in English." It's an intelligent surmise from Herbert Hoover's success in China that he understood more Chinese than he let on.

Surviving the Boxer Rebellion

Before leaving Tientsin on September 22, 1901, the Hoovers endured 28 days of siege of the city by the Boxers, who were committed to driving foreigners out of China. Throughout the ordeal, neither of the Hoovers indicated fear, though artillery shells fell all around, including five on their Racecourse Road home, and bodies could be seen floating down the Pieho River.

During the seige, food was hard to get. Mrs. Hoover became known as the one lady who could cook horsemeat better than anyone else. Their material loss was not small, as they learned when they took inventory after the siege ended.

Off to London

Herbert Hoover had just turned 27 before leaving China with Lou for the long journey back to London. Charles Algernon Moreing felt Mr. Hoover had accomplished a great deal while in China, and Herbert Hoover became a partner in Bewick, Moreing and Company in December, 1901. The firm had offices in London, Johannesburg, Tientsin, Kalgoorlie, Auckland and Tarkwa, West Africa. There was also a turquoise mine in Egypt, a silver mine in Nevada, a coal mine in

Transvaal, South Africa, and a tin mine in Cornwall, England. The real focus of their operations was in Western Australia, with the Kalgoorlie Golden Mile and other gold mines there. Consequently, Herbert Hoover traveled a great deal. In fact, he calculated that, in 1905, he traveled 32,800 miles outside England.

After arriving in England, the Hoovers rented homes in and around London. In 1902 they lived in a small home called the "White House" at Ashley Drive, Walton-on-Thames, a few miles southwest of London. The same year they rented an apartment at 39 Hyde Park Gate in London's Kensington section. It was also the home in which their two sons, Herbert Jr. and Allan, were born. For five years, it was the Hoover residence—when the family was in town.

Seven weeks after Herbert Jr. was born on August 4, 1904, he started traveling with his parents, wherever work took his father. They first went to Australia to the Kalgoorlie Golden Mile. Even after Allan's birth on July 17, 1907, the foursome traveled together, whenever feasible. Most parents would probably not consider such journeys worth the effort, but the Hoovers liked to be together as much as possible, and so world travel became a way of life.

On December 20, 1907, the Hoovers moved into the "Red House" on Hornton Street West in London's Kensington section, a house that, by 1909, cost them more than $2,000 a year in rent. It was an old, rambling, two-story house built in the 1830s. It had steam heating, large bathrooms, and an oak-panelled library with a fireplace and leaded glass bookcases. The dining room had walnut panels and a dais elevated two or three steps upon which theatrical performances could be given. The outside, surrounded by a high brick wall, had a garden, an ancient mulberry tree and a fish pond with a fountain.

Mrs. Victoria French Allen, whose husband, Ben, was with the Associated Press, never forgot the fountain after the couple's first meeting with the Hoovers. She and her husband had arrived for Sunday supper when Lou Henry said, "Come out and see Mr. Hoover and the boys. They're panning for gold in the fountain." Herbert Hoover was entertaining his sons with a prospector's pan containing ore which he had crushed with a geologist's hammer.

Holidays were special at the Red House. At Christmas, Mr. Hoover would dress as Santa Claus and distribute presents to the household staff and their children. At Easter, he would hide colored eggs in the garden to the delight of his children and his servants' children, who would hunt for them. Traditional American holidays—the Fourth of July and Thanksgiving—as well as the anniversary of California's admission to the Union were appropriately celebrated.

The Hoovers loved to entertain, and their Sunday evening suppers in their London homes, especially the Red House, drew many American mining engineers and Stanford alums and professors, as well as British guests. As one American guest later observed, the Red House became "a mecca for Californians."

Herbert Hoover remained a partner with Bewick, Moreing and Company until 1908. For the next six years, Hoover organized a group of mining engineers, including his brother, Tad, and found them assignments in the field. With the Theodore Hoovers living in London since 1906, the two couples did a great deal of motoring through the British Isles and took trips to the Continent. They loved to attend the theatre, which they frequently did. There were picnics in the parks, summers at the shore, fishing in small streams and building dams with the children in little brooks.

War comes to London

Herbert and Lou Henry Hoover and their sons were in London when World War I broke out in August 1914. So, within days, were over 100,000 American travelers who, due to an interruption in ocean transportation, were stranded there. At the urging of U.S. Ambassador Walter Hines Page, Herbert Hoover organized a group which took care of these tourist refugees. As the war developed, American Rhodes Scholars would often meet at the Red House. Before the United States entered the war in 1917, Herbert Hoover used many of these scholars in his efforts to distribute food in Belgium.

Busy with his Belgian relief work, Herbert Hoover was seldom home, but he and the rest of the family were in the Red House one night in 1916 during a German bombing run over London. "Mrs. Hoover ran to the boys' room to gather them up, intending to go into the basement, but their beds were empty," he wrote later. "We furiously searched the house from attic to basement, but no boys. It then occured to me that they sometimes climbed up a ladder through a trap door from the attic onto the roof. Pushing up the trap door, we found them calmly observing the streaming searchlights and fighting planes. We decided to join them, and behold, we witnessed a Zeppelin brought down in flames north of London. We mentally marked the direction, and, as soon as it was daylight, we got out the car and went in search of the wreck. With the help of a friendly policeman, both boys came home with treasured parts of the Zeppelin which clashed with our other household goods for years."

The Hoovers had long dreamed and talked of moving to California permanently once Herbert Hoover got out of the mining business. He had considered the academic life at Stanford. Throughout their early life together, they returned to the United States frequently, and, as often as possible, visited California, where Lou Henry's parents and sister still lived. They were drawn to the Stanford campus and rented many homes from Stanford professors for the short periods they were there.

The Hoover family successively booked and cancelled homeward passage to the U.S. on five ships. Finally, on October 3, 1914, Lou Henry and the boys sailed on the S.S. Lusitania for New York, leaving Herbert Hoover and his relief work behind. Lou Henry took her boys to California, where they lived with friends and relatives and attended school when she returned to Europe in December 1914. She remained in London until May 1915 and returned again in November with Allan and Herbert Jr. Together again, the family remained in the Red House until 1917, when they returned to the United States. The furniture was placed in storage, and, in late 1917, the Red House lease was sold.

Off to France

Herbert Hoover was traveling extensively in Europe during his Belgian relief work, which began in October 1914 and continued into March, 1920. After America entered the war, he headed the U.S. Food Administration. Later, at the Versailles peace conference, he was the U.S. representative to the Supreme Economic Council. Finally, he became chairman of the European Relief Council, a private American umbrella group that raised humanitarian aid for the children of war-stricken Europe.

While participating in the peace negotiations that followed the war, Herbert Hoover had an apartment at 19 rue de Lubeck in Paris, which was the palace of the Duc de Lubeck, pretender to the throne of France. Many of Mr. Hoover's friends stayed there when in Paris. "Madame" was the housekeeper who ran the house for Hoover.

Eventually, Mr. Hoover's duties in Europe diminished, allowing him to return to America and California, where he rejoined his family at Stanford. Just before leaving Paris, Lou Henry and their son, Allan, visited Paris and lived in the rue de Lubeck apartment.

THE RED HOUSE LONDON, ENGLAND

CHAPTER SIX:
The Lou Henry Hoover House

With Herbert Hoover back in America, the Hoovers settled at Stanford University, which they considered their residence even throughout the time Herbert Hoover was Secretary of Commerce and President of the United States, with homes in Washington, D.C. at 2300 S St. NW and the White House. Between 1914 and 1920, the Hoovers rented seven different houses in Palo Alto and Stanford for short periods of time, four different houses in Washington, D.C. and one in New York City.

In 1917 or 1918 the Hoovers engaged San Francisco architect Louis Mulgardt to design their home. When Mulgardt released this information, it was picked up by the national news wire services, which considerably upset the Hoovers. They felt it was a poor time to be publicly planning a new home and that Mulgardt was making it more pretentious than they wanted. They paid him off and dismissed him.

Plans to build their California home were delayed, but, on September 27, 1919, on his return to California, Herbert Hoover made this statement: "My family is building a 'palace' containing seven rooms and a basement, a kitchen and a garage, all on the university campus. The old cottage was good enough, but we all think we can build a better house than anybody ever built before, and every American family is entitled to this experience once in a lifetime. I offer this intimate disclosure of private affairs in order that no further inquiry on this subject will be needed and so that it may be seen that I contemplate no mischief against this commonwealth, neither actual nor even in the purview of the Federal Trade Commission."

No doubt he thought this would silence speculation about this house, so there would be no repeat of what happened earlier. This proved to be wishful thinking. When Herbert Hoover was being considered as a presidential candidate, some politician was quoted in the paper as saying, "Hoover lives in a palatial residence on his estate at Stanford University." On one of the few occasions that Herbert Hoover answered such remarks, he was quoted as saying, "This 'estate' is only one acre, and the house is a seven-room house." Birge Clark, the architect who designed the house, later rationalized this by saying, "Well, there are the two children's bedrooms on the second floor, the living room, dining room, kitchen and study and the master bedroom on the first floor." Hoover just didn't count the servants' rooms or the guest rooms on the other floors. The house cost $137,000.

Lou Henry and Herbert Hoover chose as the site for their new home a hill on the Stanford campus where they used to sit, enjoy the view and perhaps court and have a pleasant time together before they were married. It showed their strong thread of sentiment and feeling for one another that ran through their lives and, in turn, a feeling for Stanford. When Herbert Hoover came back from Europe, the land was vacant. He leased it from the university and built the house on the spot that afforded a view from his study they both liked.

The Hoovers selected Arthur B. Clark and his son, Birge M. Clark, as their architects. Since Arthur, head of Stanford's Art Department, was very busy and his son had just returned from the service, the main planning fell upon Birge. "Every now and then you have a man who wants his wife to have what she wants in a house," Birge Clark once said. "He's happy if she's happy, but he is not going to devote himself to the detail of planning. Mr. Hoover was something like this and paid no attention. She tried to involve him, but he was spending most of the time in Washington and Europe and seemed interested in the house mainly because of Mrs. Hoover's interest. The both wanted it to be a 'home in keeping with the two-story faculty homes in the neighborhood of San Juan Hill,' and a considerably smaller house than it turned out to be. But, as often happens in architectural practice, an owner has various hard-core components and needs and just doesn't realize at first how much space their assembly is going to encompass.

"Though Mr. Hoover paid no attention, Mrs. Hoover paid a great deal of attention, far more than the average client ever would," he said. "She had excellent taste, with complete confidence in her taste. Neither of them wanted the house to be a French Provincial, an English Manor, early California, or any historical style. They just wanted it to be a house."

An article in the February, 1929, issue of Western Homes and Gardens describes the Hoovers' home on San Juan Hill of the Stanford University campus like this: "At first glance the exterior of this residence suggests the Pueblo influence, but a closer study of the various elevations reveals the true motif, the Algerian, with every roof an outdoor living room, accessible by a staircase. The site is a hillside with a fine view of the famous Santa Clara Valley and an intimate association for its owners with the halls of learning where they met and from which they graduated; the house itself is a mass of piled up blocks with terraces, outer staircases and fireplaces everywhere inviting freedom and comfort. A dignified unpretentiousness prevails."

Arthur Clark expressed the final design of the house very well: "The prevailing spirit of the house is one of extreme livableness and utter lack of formality and ostentation, the individuality of the owner being evidenced everywhere by the lack of conventionality and disregard of tradition or the accepted ways of doing things."

Birge Clark said he knew Herbert Hoover liked the house because he had told him so, but he never heard him express any great delight with it. "At the time when the cove living room ceiling had been finished and was being painted, he (Herbert Hoover) arrived home, and Mrs. Hoover asked me to come over and meet them both at the house. They were both moving around, and Mrs. Hoover was explaining things, and, if he asked a question she couldn't answer, he would turn to me. The second-story ceiling over the stair hall had just been 'glazed' with an 'antique finish.' This was the last of several experiments, and Mrs. Hoover had thought it was just about right. Mr. Hoover looked at it and said, 'Well, I saw some basements in Belgium that looked worse than that,' so Mrs. Hoover said, 'We won't antique anything from here on.'

"Then she told him about the living room ceiling and how it was attaining a soft general light without any visible source. Mr. Hoover smiled again and said, 'Well, it looks kind of like early Pullman to me.' This was the only time that I ever saw Mrs. Hoover express any irritableness with her husband: 'Bert, it

THE LOU HENRY HOOVER HOUSE, PALO ALTO, CALIFORNIA

does not.' And later that day she phoned me just to say that 'Mr. Hoover was merely making a little joke to tease me, and he really thought the living room ceiling was just fine.' I am sure that was the case, as while Mr. Hoover had a rather dry, though gentle, sense of humor, I never heard him say anything which really hurt anyone's feelings, although this time he certainly irritated his wife."

A secret room, secret stairs and secret panels

Birge Clark recalls, too, that the Hoovers' Stanford home contained a second-floor "secret room," Lou Henry's study: "There was a very steep winding 'secret stairs' from her dressing room that led to it," he said. "When she was in that room, she was theoretically out of the house and no one should know where she is. She had her writing desk in front of the three little windows that looked out on Reservoir Drive and at the entrance so, if she saw somebody coming who she wanted to see, she could run down the stairs or phone down and tell whoever might answer the bell to bring them in; otherwise, a servant would merely say that Mrs. Hoover was out and no one knew where. She was very friendly so probably didn't take advantage of this very often; however, this was the day when ladies left cards, and there may well have been people that Mrs. Hoover was satisfied to let do only that."

The dining room was patterned after the one in the London Red House, with the raised dais. Whether many theatricals were given in either room is difficult to say. Another feature of this dining room was the secret panels in the walls. Herbert Hoover was once showing a group of his wife's friends around the house, and, when they came to the dining room, asked, "Does anybody have a hairpin?" No one did, so he found a paper clip and straightened it. He inserted the paper clip in tiny, invisible holes in the panels of the walls, opening secret doors all around the dining room to display his wife's collection of beautiful pewter. He jokingly commented, "This is the only collection my wife has of which I really and truly approve, because it doesn't cost very much." That was yesteryear—prices of pewter have gone up.

In a letter to Birge Clark written while the house was being built, Lou Henry told him to make a secret panel of the door to the closet in the living room under the brick stairway leading to the second floor, as she didn't think a regular door would look nice there. The whole idea of these secret panels was not one of secrecy, but simply a dislike for hinges and door knobs. All of these secret panels could be opened with a hat pin, so there were always hat pins on the dining room mantel, the study mantel and often on the ledge at the top of the paneling, as in the case of the fairly large closet door in the living room.

Fireplaces, inside and out

Lou Henry Hoover loved fireplaces. Her new Stanford home had fireplaces in every principal room, as well as outside on the terrace for toasting marshmallows or weiners. During the first winter in the new house, ashes from the entry hall blew out onto the floor when the front door was left open. "The ashes can be swept up," Lou Henry Hoover said. "I am not going to give up fires in the fireplaces because a few ashes blow out."

She not only enjoyed the fires, but she knew what to do about fireplaces when anything went wrong. On March 9, 1939, the Hoovers were the dinner guests of the Thomas Deweys at their home at 1148 Fifth Avenue, New York City. He was a lawyer and would later become governor of New York and a candidate for president. During dinner, the fireplace began to smoke, and the Deweys were embarrassed. Mrs. Hoover left the table and casually adjusted the damper to stop the outpour of smoke.

The Stanford house was finished about June of 1920, and the Hoover family moved in. When the furniture from the London Red House had been taken from storage, the Hoovers found shipping and water damage. A large Oriental rug had large dark stains. "I never liked the color of that rug anyway," Lou Henry said, "and now will be as good a time as any to have it dyed dark, and the dark stains will be minimized." The rug was shipped off to a dyeing and cleaning firm, and, when it came back, all the light areas were a fairly soft brown and, of course, the reds and blues were greatly darkened. As Birge Clark described it, "The whole rug was more or less a monochrome, rather than a mutichrome."

Birge Clark remembers an Armenian rug dealer coming to the house to appraise the rugs. When he came to the big rug, he began mumbling and got down on his hands and knees and turned the rug over and moved from side to side, feeling it. "I have never seen a rug like this," he said. "I do not understand it." Birge Clark explained, "Well, you see the stains were so dark they could not be cleaned out, so Mrs. Hoover had it dyed." The appraiser recoiled violently and said, "She had the rug dyed? An Oriental rug? I never heard of such a thing. Of course it could have been cleaned." Birge Clark said he realized that Herbert Hoover had lost the Armenian rug dealer's vote right then.

Thanks to Mildred Campbell Hall we have a glimpse of a few of Lou Henry Hoover's decorating ideas for her Stanford home. After Lou Henry's death in 1944, Herbert Hoover gave his wife's former secretary a pair of green, cloisonné type bowls that Mildred Campbell Hall remembers sat in the Stanford house on the steps going from the living room to the dining room. The Peruvian silver bowls—nine or 10 inches across the mouth and decorated with little birds—had been brought back by the Hoovers from their South American goodwill trip from November, 1928 to January, 1929. Another gift was a big brass plaque decorated with tigers, elephants and other Indian animals that once hung in the front hall of the Stanford house.

A car in the basement

Herbert Jr. and Allan Hoover once built a car in the basement, using a motorcycle engine. Once finished, the car couldn't be removed, except through a window. Lou Henry Hoover climbed into the car, which had a small plank for a seat, and drove it around the campus. Both parents entered into their boys' activities and had great fun with them.

The Stanford house had a swimming pool. There were many swimming parties, and the Hoovers' secretaries were free to invite their friends. Those who did not arrive in swimming suits were free to use the downstairs guest rooms as dressing rooms. A student was employed as a life guard to see that nobody drowned. There was also a rule that no child could go in unless the student guard or an adult was present.

When living in Stanford, Lou Henry maintained a neighborly atmosphere, inviting professors' wives in for informal teas and going around San Juan Hill, yoo hooing in kitchen windows or casually dropping by. Neighbors were used to seeing the Hoovers going past their houses for a pre-breakfast stroll when Herbert Hoover was home.

In 1921, when his parents spent most of their time in Washington, D.C., Herbert Jr. lived in the San Juan Hill house while attending Stanford. There was always someone living in the house to keep things going and to look after the boys in between Lou Henry's visits.

The "dearest spot on earth"

After Lou Henry's death in 1944, Herbert Hoover lived in New York City. He presented the Stanford house as a gift to the university. Named the Lou Henry Hoover House, it is used as a residence for Stanford presidents. There was a period in the late 1940s and early 1950s when Herbert Hoover would spend several weeks at the house. Usually, the president of Stanford would be conveniently off on vacation at the time, so Herbert Hoover had the place completely to himself. Boris, his valet, would be there to look after him. He also had an office on campus in the Hoover Tower, where he worked during the day.

Since he didn't like to eat alone, Herbert Hoover would often invite guests to dinner, usually in groups of eight that mainly included old-timers on the campus and former neighbors who knew Lou Henry. A banker friend, Harold H. Helm, recalls that after dinner on one such occasion Herbert Hoover went into the yard, asking any of the group to come along if they wished. He was poking around in the garden and shrubbery, pointing out, "I remember when Mrs. Hoover planted that." As Helm expressed it, "He gave every indication of feeling that this was about the dearest spot on earth to him, to be in that home and in that garden. The affectionate way he spoke of the way the house was built and the plans that were made for it made you realize that he and Mrs. Hoover must have been a very happy couple and must have thoroughly enjoyed their residency in their Palo Alto house."

In 1968, when the university undertook the renovation and modernization of the Lou Henry Hoover House, Birge Clark remarked that he "was sure Mrs. Hoover would be delighted that I am still being involved in altering the house on which she 'acted as the architect,' and it demonstrated one of her firmest beliefs about houses—that they are never finished, but are a living entity bridging generations, and often being altered and added to, to suit changing conditions."

The Lou Henry Hoover House was designated as a national landmark by the U.S. Department of the Interior on April 29, 1985.

CHAPTER SEVEN:
The Washington years

When the United States entered World War I, Herbert Hoover was appointed the nation's Food Administrator and the Hoovers began their long association with Washington, D.C. Over six years beginning in 1915, they lived in five different rented homes and in two Washington hotels. From 1921 and 1927, when Mr. Hoover served as Secretary of Commerce under two presidents—Warren G. Harding and Calvin Coolidge—they lived in their own home at 2300 S St. NW. It was this spacious house at the foot of 23rd and S streets, high above the street and approachable by steps, that the Hoovers considered their home away from Stanford.

Even though the Hoovers still considered the Stanford University campus their official residence, they had many good friends among their neighbors and co-workers in Washington. Lou Henry Hoover and Grace Coolidge became close friends during this time, cultivating a friendship that lasted a lifetime. Neighbors included the Adolph Millers (he was an economist and a governor of the Federal Reserve Board), the Eugene Meyers (another governor of the Federal Reserve Board who held various government posts under Presidents Harding, Coolidge and Hoover), the Arthur Bullards (who remained long-time family friends), the Edgar Rickards (Herbert Hoover's financial adviser and former relief assistant) and the Mark Sullivans (Herbert Hoover received criticism for being such a close friend of this prominent newspaper columnist).

The general reports picture the Hoovers' S Street residence as comfortable and in good taste. The candid viewpoints and remembrances of two of the Sullivan children show they had other ideas. Sydney thought the house big and comfortable, but tasteless and uninteresting. To Mark Jr.'s mind, the Hoovers were right squirrely—the house seemed overcrowded with items brought back from the Far East. There were boxes, figurines, carved quartz and plaques from Belgium all over the tables. It was a bad experience for a young boy, "because you were always likely to bump a table and knock 25 things onto the floor, and you'd worry about what you've broken this time," Mark said. "It was pretty hard to move across the room without bumping into something." It's little wonder, as Sydney noted, "We were occasionally told to look at magazines."

Mildred Hall Campbell, who was Lou Henry's secretary, remembers the Hoovers' S Street home as "a dream of a place for solid comfort, with beautiful and intriguing objects d'art from all over the world, but an atmosphere of hominess prevailed the whole." The routine at S Street, she recalled, included Herbert Hoover arriving home in the late afternoon. "We all met on the long veranda which opened onto the back garden," she said. "Tall orange juice drinks were brought out by Ellis, the butler, and everybody gave an account of himself and his adventures for the day. No question was too foolish for Mr. Hoover to answer. He would listen with that amused twinkle in his eye. He was a quiet man, but not withdrawn, with no forced, artificial, sophisticated chatter."

Parties, big and small

The Hoovers were very hospitable and had many guests at their S Street home. Herbert Hoover would have men come in for breakfast, and he and

2300 S STREET NW   WASHINGTON, D.C.

Lou Henry would have guests for dinner practically every night. Usually they didn't consider it entertaining, just time spent with intimate groups.

There were large gatherings, too, some impromptu. One year Grace Coolidge, Lou Henry's predecessor as First Lady, was ill and unable to receive the Daughters of the American Revolution, so Lou Henry was asked to receive them. She and the head officers of the DAR hosted about 1,500 DAR members on one afternoon at the S Street residence. Guests went in the front door, through the receiving line, and out through Herbert Hoover's den. They were shown the gold box that had been given him by the Belgians and told about the different things in his den. They went out on the porch and down into the garden. There were tables with punch and cookies served by DAR members. They left by the garden gate. How the police handled the traffic problem was not reported, but after the party Lou Henry and those who helped gathered in the living room for refreshments and discussion of the afternoon. Lou Henry was very happy and very pleased with how it was done and how many came.

In preparation for another party, the secretaries were trying to decorate the porch of the S Street house with flowers. They weren't satisfied, and Herbert Hoover wasn't satisfied. Lou Henry was in New York and not due back until 11 in the morning for the afternoon party. Herbert Hoover showed them how to fix the flowers by putting them in groups in the different corners of the porch. The result was beautiful, and everyone was satisified and happy he had had a part in making it so.

The S Street house had 22 rooms, requiring 11 domestic helpers to take care of it. Mary Rattley did all the cooking, and, as Gertrude Bowman, a secretary, reported, "Everything was perfect. She was an excellent cook, and no extra people were brought in, even when they entertained the Coolidges and the Hardings. Mary would see that the food went upstairs on the dumbwaiter and was taken care of by Leon and Ellis. It was beautifully presented and decorated and garnished. The servants wanted to do everything the way Mrs. Hoover wanted to run the house, and were pleased with the salaries that they received, and the holidays and other privileges they were given."

Mildred "Mindy" Hoover Willis, who was Herbert Hoover's niece, once visited the S Street house with her husband, Cornelius. They were quartered in a lovely room with a large double bed. Since she was a restless sleeper, her husband decided he would be more comfortable elsewhere. He had seen a narrow cot just down the hall, so he took a blanket and pillow and went out there to sleep. When the masseur arrived early the next morning, Herbert Hoover was surprised to find his niece's husband sound asleep on his rubbing table.

Some of the neighbors wanted the Hoovers to sign a petition, promising they wouldn't sell their S Street home to Negroes or Jews. Both the Hoovers and the Sullivans refused. The house was sold in 1944, the year Lou Henry died at age 69, for $87,250. In 1953, it was bought by the government of Burma for $150,000 and is now known as the Burmese Embassy.

CHAPTER EIGHT:
1600 Pennsylvania Avenue

The Hoovers' next home belonged to the people of the United States. The White House is a home many men, but few wives, aspire to. However, once they are there, they enter zestfully into the tasks before them.

The president and his wife have a regular schedule of official entertaining. The Diplomatic Reception is the most brilliant of the season, due in part to the colorful clothing worn by representatives of various nations. There are also receptions for the departments of government, dinners for the president's cabinet and the vice president and other affairs for visiting heads of state.

As in all their other homes, the Hoovers had many guests in the White House. Family dinners were held with their old S Street neighbors—the Mark Sullivans and Adolph Millers—the Vernon Kellogs and many others. U.S. Army General John Pershing, American Red Cross Secretary Mabel Broadman and Mary Vaux Walcott, widow of Smithsonian Institution Director Charles D. Walcott, were there several times together. Des Moines Register cartoonist J. N. "Ding" Darling was a house guest, as Herbert Hoover enjoyed his cartoons so much. Of course, the Jeremiah Milbanks and other many close friends were often White House guests, too.

Susan Dyer, a family friend, recalls a White House Christmas dinner attended by cabinet members and their families. As the dinner concluded, the waiters brought bells for the gentlemen and candlesticks for the ladies. The lights were turned down, and the gentlemen lit the candles. Leaving the State Dining Room, the dinner guests walked down the corridor to the East Room, the gentlemen ringing their bells. Herbert Hoover later gave Susan Dyer the bell he carried that night.

A Christmas Eve fire

Turner Catledge of the New York Times recalls that Richard V. Oulahan, chief of the paper's Washington Bureau, came by the desk and dropped off his copy, saying, "This is my story for the day. I am going home and have Christmas Eve with my children. Don't call me unless the White House burns." An hour later, Catledge called. "Mr. Oulahan," he said, "the White House in on fire."

On that Christmas Eve in 1929, as the Hoovers were hosting a Christmas party for the children of the White House staff and other friends, the executive office area of the West Wing of the White House caught fire. Among the other guests at the party was radio entertainer Charles Field, known as "Cheerio" due to his broadcasts of happy philosophy at the breakfast hour. The guests, including eight small sons and daughters of the president's secretaries and personal physician, were gathered around a table in the State Dining Room having a delightful time when Lawrence Richey, the president's secretary, was told of the fire. He left the table to check and returned to tell Herbert Hoover, whose happy expression instantly disappeared. All the men at the party, except "Cheerio," withdrew.

"Cheerio" stayed behind to help Lou Henry Hoover, who had experienced many emergencies, carry the party through to its close in a manner gracious and serene. The U.S. Marine Corps Band played on and on at her request as the children were transferred from the State Dining Room to the East Room. Then, Lou Henry disappeared. When she returned, she called the children around her. She explained to them why their fathers had left; they had to go because their offices were on fire. She asked the children if they would like to go up to the second story to see the smoke. Would they? Eight pairs of scampering feet were the answer. Soon, eight young faces were pressed close to the panes of a cathedral-like window at the end of the great upper hall.

What they saw was exciting to them, but a nightmare to everyone else. The fire had been discovered soon after 8 p.m. by W.W. Rice, a switchboard operator in the basement of the Executive Office Building just west of the White House. By 10:40 p.m., practically all the fire-fighting apparatus in Washington, D.C. had responded to the three alarms and had extinguished the fire. The night was so cold that the spray from the fire hoses froze as it fell, glazing the courtyard and walls of the building and making the work of firemen hazardous.

Presidential secretaries Lawrence Richey and George Akerson and the President's son, Allan, who was home from college, braved the smoke to rescue some of Herbert Hoover's personal files and other documents. Later, they saved the chairs used by the President and members of his cabinet at cabinet meetings. The three of them soon had plenty of helpers, although Herbert Hoover was persuaded to watch from a safe distance. George Akerson had bought his son, George Jr., who was watching from the great upper hall, a little wire-haired terrier as a Christmas gift and had left it in a cage in his office. In the excitement, Akerson forgot the dog, but Herbert Hoover remembered it and directed firemen to go in and rescue the terrier.

The damage estimate for the building and its furnishings was at least $60,000. Fire and water had destroyed some valuable documents of secretaries and newspaper correspondents, but there were no reports of injuries. All were grateful it had not been worse and that the White House proper had been spared. Defective wiring was blamed for the disaster. Plans were immediately underway for conducting business as usual, with offices being set up in the White House and at the State, War and Navy Building across the street until the West Wing office areas were ready for occupancy again.

The next Christmas, the Hoovers gave the children gifts to remind them of the fire. The boys received iron fire engines, painted red. The girls received lovely little jewelry boxes made of wood which had been saved from the offices damaged by the fire.

A controversial tea party

On many winter afternoons Lou Henry Hoover would have four or five tea parties going on in four or five different rooms of the White House, enjoying them all. After Oscar De Priest, a black Republican politician from Chicago, was elected to Congress, Lou Henry Hoover invited his wife, Jessie, to a White House tea. Lou Henry also invited her sister, Jean, and the wives of other Congressmen, "selecting them," according to a secretary, Mildred Hall, "on the basis of her knowing how they would feel in such a picture." Mildred Hall remembers that the Hoovers' black butler, Ellis, seemed both surprised and delighted as he passed the tea cakes. She said it meant a great deal to him to see a woman of his race being entertained in the Green Room of the White House by the wife of the President of the United States.

A flood of abusive letters followed that June 12, 1929, tea party. It was unfortunate for Lou Henry that she opened and read them. But she stood her ground. She had done the right thing, and she knew it.

Lou Henry Hoover's abilities as a gracious hostess who made those around her feel at ease extended to contacts with total strangers. She was once hosting a White House tea for some Girl Scout board members, and two little girls heard about it and headed to the White House to learn more about becoming Girl Scouts. They arrived before the tea began, and Lou Henry received them and graciously explained the Girl Scout movement to them.

Dr. Levi Pennington, a prominent Quaker who was president of Pacific College in Oregon during the Hoover presidency, tells of Lou Henry shopping on one occasion. A woman at the same counter said to her, "Aren't you Mrs. Hoover, the President's wife?" Assured she was right, the woman said, "This will be a red letter day for me. I was shopping alongside the wife of the President of the United States." With one of her lovely smiles, Lou Henry said, "Well, let's make it as much worthwhile as we can," so she held out her hand and shook hands with her fellow customer, and they chatted for awhile as any two chance acquaintances might.

"I have said many times that Mrs. Hoover was as near to being a perfect hostess as any woman I have ever know," Dr. Pennington said. "I believe that she would have had the queen of England, an Irish washerwoman and a Negro 'mammy' as guests together and all three of them feeling at home and having a happy time as guests of the President's wife."

Early morning workouts

The White House grounds became a recreation area during the Hoovers' stay at 1600 Pennsylvania Avenue. On March 4, 1929, the day of his inauguration, Herbert Hoover weighed over 200 pounds. After what a friend, author Will Irwin, termed a "serious little talk" with his personal physician, Dr. Joel Boone, Herbert Hoover decided to begin every day with an early-morning round of "bull in the ring," a strenuous game that involves tossing and catching a nine-pound medicine ball. Regular players included U.S. Supreme Court Justice Harlan Stone, Secretary of the Interior Ray Lyman Wilbur, Attorney General William DeWitt Mitchell, Secretary of Agriculture Arthur Hyde and Assistant Secretary of the Treasury Walter Hope.

"Four days after the inauguration, they reported in old clothes and sweaters on the White House lawn and went merrily to it," Will Irwin wrote in 1931. Before long, Irwin said, boredom prompted "bull in the ring" to be replaced by a new game invented by Dr. Boone. It combined medicine ball and lawn tennis to produce a hybrid team sport akin to volleyball. It was played with a six-pound medicine ball on a 30-by-66 foot court divided by a net eight feet high.

"When the game worked itself into form, the White House staff marked five courts: three out-of-doors and two indoors," Irwin wrote. "The latter were intended for rainy or snowy days... At seven o'clock sharp, they choose partners and begin. Usually, they play doubles, two on a side. Sometimes, when the attendance is heavy, they vary this with 'triples.' This arrangement, impossible for lawn tennis, only adds liveliness to the new game. A factory down by the Potomac blows a loud whistle at seven-thirty. This is the signal to quit, no matter how close the score, for the business of governing must go on. By this time, the players are usually in a reeking perspiration."

The game, which Irwin described as "more strenuous than either boxing, wrestling or football," helped keep Herbert Hoover, who was 5-foot-11, under 185 pounds. "I couldn't get along without steady exercise now," Herbert Hoover said in 1931. "When you've started, you must keep it up."

Architectural advice

While in the Washington, D.C., Lou Henry Hoover was far removed from the San Juan Hill house at Stanford that she had helped design. But she was still able to share her architectural insights with members of her White House staff. Phillips and Katurah Brooks, a couple that worked as servants for the Hoovers in Washington, took Lou Henry's advice when they built a home.

"Katurah, if you ever decide to build a house, be sure to have your kitchen on the southern exposure," Lou Henry once told Katurah Brooks. "You get the sun all day. It come up and it comes over and you get it in your kitchen all day."

"And we did," Katurah said. "That kitchen was the coolest in the summer and the warmest in the winter. We get part of the sun all day."

A furnishings inventory

One of Lou Henry Hoover's White House projects has come to light only in recent years. With the help of several secretaries, especially Dare McMullin, she made an effort to catalog the furnishings of the White House. Using catalog cards and a three-way cross reference system, each piece was assigned a number and was cataloged by a) administration, b) object and c) location.

Lou Henry felt each piece catalogued should be photographed, and she insisted on paying for the photographs herself. It was her contention that the Hoovers would pay for everything they would take with them when they left the White House. When U.S. Grant III, director of Public Buildings and Public Parks of the National Capitol, insisted that the government foot the bill, Lou Henry finally gave in to his wishes.

Deciding that catalog cards would not make for interesting reading, Lou Henry decided a chronicle of their findings should be developed. Work on the catalog and the narrative began in 1930 and continued until the Hoovers left the White House the first week of March, 1933. The writing project was not funded, and it was left to Dare McMullin to find a publisher. This she was unable to do. In the meantime, U.S. Grant III presented a bill for photographs. Lou Henry paid the bill, but felt she had been ill-used, since from the beginning she had wanted it handled another way.

This valuable piece of White House research was years in surfacing. Jacqueline Kennedy had heard only rumors of its existence and was never able to make use of it in her White House furnishings project while First Lady. Lou Henry's narrative, which Mrs. Kennedy and others felt would have been most help-

THE WHITE HOUSE, 1600 PENNSYLVANIA AVENUE
WASHINGTON, D.C.

ful, is displayed at the Herbert Hoover Presidential Library and Museum in West Branch.

Lou Henry's furnishings catalog project didn't involve the acquisition of furniture, only the recording of what was in the White House, even in the basement. There was one exception—Monroe-period furniture that had been disposed of. Lou Henry had copies of several pieces of Monroe furniture made for the Rose Room. With the approval of a committee that approves any change in White House furnishings, Lou Henry gave the Monroe-period reproductions to the White House as her going away present.

CHAPTER NINE:
An oasis in the mountains

The White House has a tendency to give presidents cabin fever. Some have rented a place some distance from Washington, some have had the government build a place in the mountains and some went to their own retreats, however far away. The Hoovers wanted a mosquito-free place about 100 miles from Washington, where "The Chief" could fish, "The Lady" could enjoy horseback riding and both could escape the sweltering summer heat of the capital.

Dr. Joel T. Boone, Herbert Hoover's personal physician, was convinced that such a retreat was vital to maintaining the President's health and was an important reason why Herbert Hoover endured four years in the White House without serious illness.

"He and his highly intelligent and wonderful wife were devotees of the great outdoors, wanting to be closely a part of it," Dr. Boone later wrote in reflecting on the Hoovers' need for a retreat. "They had traveled and lived in many parts of the world and knew that with all the challenges of his office and subjected to constant pounding of activity and the heaviest kind of omnipresent pressures, he must find a place, not too far away from Washington, where he could relax and enjoy in as much quietude as possible the blessings of nature."

After a horseback survey into the Blue Ridge Mountains of Virginia with Dr. Boone and others, the Hoovers selected a 164-acre site between the Laurel and Mill Prongs, which carried mountain waters to the Rapidan River. Marine Corps engineers who developed the site diverted the prong waters somewhat to form Hemlock Run, which flows near the site of the President's cabin.

The Hoovers foot the bill

Although Congress appropriated $48,000 in 1928 to pay for conversion of a Weather Bureau station at Bluemont, Virginia, into a summer White House in the mountains, President-elect Herbert Hoover refused to spend the money. When the state of Virginia later offered to build a $100,000 Presidential Lodge, Herbert Hoover declined that offer, too. Instead, on July 31, 1929, he used his personal funds to pay the prevailing price of $5 an acre for the 164-acre site. Another 2,000 acres surrounding the site were leased for protection and privacy and for use as hiking trails and bridle paths. By the time development of the retreat known as "Rapidan" was completed, Herbert Hoover had spent $114,000 in personal funds on Rapidan during his four-year term, according to his accountants.

The first structure to be erected at the camp was known as "Five Tents," an appropriate name for the five brown canvas tents pitched side-by-side over a wooden floor. Herbert Hoover spent his first night at Camp Rapidan on May 18, 1929, under one of those tents. Once completed, the camp complex included 12 rustic buildings constructed in open-beam style, including the President's lodge, two mess halls, cottages for presidential aides, guest cabins and a central building known as "Town Hall." The "Brown House," as the President's lodge was first known, had a 60-by-20-foot living room, two bedrooms, two bathrooms, a screened sleeping porch and a large sitting porch. The lodge was built with two fireplaces, the largest, the Marines boasted, requiring 51 tons of fieldstones.

Camp Rapidan's fireplaces were its only sources of heat. An information sheet Lou Henry Hoover posted in every cabin along with maps of the camp gave this advice for enduring the coldest nights: "After all blankets and eiders are exhausted, put on your camel's hair dressing gown, wrap your head in a sweater, and throw your fur coat over everything!" Herbert Hoover apparently didn't mind the cold. "It is desirable," he once said, "that the President of the United States should be periodically reminded of this fact—that the forces of nature discriminate for no man."

As much as possible, the area was left in its natural state. The President's lodge was shoehorned in among the trees, and, at Herbert Hoover's request, a big tree was left growing through the floor of the lodge's large sitting porch. When a fountain was built, water was piped from a nearby stream, but, at Lou Henry Hoover's insistence, workers had to carefully replace rocks and vegetation disturbed to install the pipeline. Conservation was the rule at Rapidan; only dead wood was burned for cooking and heating, never living trees, coal or oil.

"Of course she was sort of opinionated," Marine Corps Major General W.W. Rogers said later of Lou Henry in remembering her from the days when he was a Captain assigned to Rapidan. "She wanted things like she wanted them, and that's what we were there for, to do things like they wanted them, so we tried to do the best we could."

Filipino cooks and servants, as well as kitchen equipment, silverware, china and furniture, were transfered from the U.S. Navy's presidential yacht, Mayflower, for use at Rapidan. The Marines built the beds used at Rapidan by Herbert and Lou Henry Hoover as well as many other pieces of sturdy furniture. Lou Henry bought braided rugs from a local woman. She also bought chairs made at the Clore furniture plant in nearby Madison, Virginia, ordering two "minus bottoms" so that she and a niece could try their hand at weaving the seats. Other furnishings were gifts, including a bowl made from hand-hewn Phillipine hardwood and a tomahawk that was mounted over a fireplace. Col. Charles Lindbergh's gift of a parchment map-lampshade showing the route of his historic trans-Altantic flight was used in Camp Rapidan's Town Hall.

A lengthy guest list

"Lucky Lindy" and his wife, Ann Morrow Lindbergh, were frequent guests at the Rapidan Camp. Lindbergh, like Herbert Hoover, enjoyed trout fishing and was frequently the winner of the camp's horseshoe pitching contests. A complete list of Rapidan guests during Herbert Hoover's term in the White House would include thousands of names, among them Winston Churchill and Thomas A. Edison. World attention was focused on the camp in October, 1929, when British Prime Minister Ramsay MacDonald and his daughter, Ishbel, visited Rapidan. During their stay Herbert Hoover and Ramsay MacDonald held a legendary discussion of naval disarmament during which it was said they dismantled the navies of the world while perched at opposite ends of a fallen tree.

Rapidan was the scene in 1931 of a crucial discussion of the mission and budget of the War Department involving the Secretary of War, the Chief and

THE BROWN HOUSE AT CAMP RAPIDAN
MADISON COUNTY, VIRGINIA

Deputy Chief of Staff and other top government officials. Members of the Supreme Court, the Cabinet and dozens of Republican congressmen and senators were also guests at Rapidan. During the summer of 1930, it was a honeymoon haven for Senator and Mrs. Reed Smoot and other newlyweds.

Many guests, like Charles Lindbergh, enjoyed fishing at Rapidan. Herbert Hoover was also fond of piling up rocks in the streams to form pools for the trout. When he wasn't catching fish, he was showing them off. After getting lost outside Fredericksburg and stopping for a picnic lunch and a nap, Lou Henry arrived late one day at Rapidan with a carful of friends. They scarcely had time to shower when they were asked to come to the Town Hall for tea. Herbert Hoover was waiting for them and said, "I promised to show you my fish." He gathered up a handful of sandwiches, prompting Lou Henry to remind him that "fish don't eat cheese." He wasn't daunted, saying, "Of course they won't eat cheese, but they won't know it's cheese, and they'll come up and that's all I want. We just want to see them."

A mountain schoolhouse

Although security at Rapidan was tight, there was an uninvited guest, too. On August 10, 1929, Herbert Hoover's 55th birthday, an 11-year-old boy named William McKinley Burraker who lived on the mountain above the camp appeared with a live opossum he had brought in a cage as a birthday gift for the President. Herbert Hoover opted not to eat the opossum, instead turning it over to his animal-loving son, Allan, who made it the camp pet. When Herbert Hoover asked his young uninvited birthday guest if he went to school, he was told there was no school. It was then the President decided to do something about this need. He solicited his friends for the money needed to build and equip a one-room schoolhouse that included an apartment for the teacher.

Herbert Hoover wrote to President Hutchins of Berea College in Kentucky, asking him to recommend a teacher. His choice was Christine Vest of Yosemite, Kentucky, who accepted the position in December, 1929. The school building was completed, and classes began in February, 1930, with an enrollment of 17. The children were fascinated by being able to turn a faucet and have water come out; they had never seen anything like that.

Christine Vest once asked Lou Henry Hoover what she thought of the idea of taking the children to the Madison County Fair. Many of the children had never been off the mountain before. She not only thought it a fine idea, but provided money for the children to buy what they wanted at the fair. The children's teacher would let Lou Henry know their needs and clothing sizes, and Lou Henry always gave them practical gifts as well as toys at Christmas time.

Lou Henry Hoover was always full of energy and once took Ann Morrow Lindbergh to the top of the mountain, where the schoolhouse was located. In introducing her guest, Lou Henry was greeted by a little boy's baffled expression. "Oh, you know Mrs. Lindbergh. You know Charles Lindbergh," Lou Henry said. The boy said, "I never heard of him." Mrs. Hoover asked, "Don't you ever get down off this mountain?" He said, "Oh yes, I've been down as far as the camp where the President goes." "What do you think of it?," Lou Henry asked. "Tain't much," he replied.

The beginnings of Skyline Drive

The Hoovers were concerned about the poverty of the mountain people, and Herbert Hoover was able to provide them with work after the Shenandoah Valley's terrible drought in 1932. On the morning after the Camp Rapidan dedication ceremony, Herbert Hoover took an early-morning horseback ride with Lou Henry, National Park Service Director Horace Albright and others. He stopped along a high ridge. "You know, this mountain is made by God Almighty for a highway," he said. "There's nothing like it in the country, really, where you can see such vistas first on one side and then the other, sometimes both ways. I think we should have a survey made here."

When Horace Albright pointed out the goverment didn't own the land, Herbert Hoover's reply was, "Virginia is very cooperative. Why don't you talk to (Virginia Conservation Department head William E.) Carson and see what you can work out. Get a survey crew in here and see what you can make out."

"The Chief" was reminded that, if a road was built, it would be the end of the Rapidan Camp's seclusion. "Of course the tourists will come right down in my yard," he said. "But, after all, I have no right to tie up a place like this. I may not be down there, and, even if I was, I'd take the chance."

He saw the road construction as a chance for jobs for the local residents. "Employ those drought-stricken farmers and don't bring in a lot of heavy equipment," he said. "Use their plows and horses and get as much money as you can back in there where it is needed." That was the beginning of Skyline Drive.

The demise of Rapidan

Herbert Hoover's loss to Franklin D. Roosevelt in the 1932 election ended the Hoovers' association with Camp Rapidan. After he left the White House Herbert Hoover deeded the camp to the federal government, and it was later incorporated into the Shenandoah National Park. Despite the addition of ramps for his wheelchair, President Roosevelt found the terrain rough going and used Rapidan as a retreat only once before ordering that another retreat be built in Maryland's Catoctin Mountains, a hideaway now known as "Camp David." As Herbert Hoover had hoped, the Boy Scouts of America used Rapidan as a camp for a time, but abandoned it because of the high costs of maintenance. Eventually, many of the cabins and even the nearby schoolhouse were torn down. Three of the orginal 12 buildings were restored in the early 1960s.

"Camp Hoover," as it was later known, was frequently used by Cabinet members and other officials of the Nixon Administration. Richard Nixon never stayed there, prefering Camp David, Key Biscayne, Florida, or his Western White House at San Clemente, California. Twice the camp was prepared for visits by Richard Nixon, who wanted to use the television in the main cabin to watch Washington Redskin football games that were blacked out on Washington television. Although those visits were canceled, the Secret Service communications equipment installed during the Nixon administration remains in place should another president one day opt to visit the fishing camp.

CHAPTER TEN:
High above Manhattan

After the 1932 election, the Hoovers returned to California and their San Juan Hill home at Stanford University. Although Herbert Hoover was in Washington much of the time, Lou Henry spent a significant amount of time each year out west. The house was the site of many affairs benefiting students and other functions, such as the Stanford Mothers Club Chrysanthemum Tea. Lou Henry was frequently seen motoring through the foothills in her little Ford roadster, often with students in the rumble seat.

Herbert Hoover's activities prompted the decision to move to New York City in 1934. Much of their furniture and furnishings were divided among their two sons and others. They brought to Manhattan only what they wanted and needed in their suite on the 16th floor of the Waldorf-Astoria Towers, which, for the next 10 years, was home at varying times.

When Margaret Nevins, a maid, heard that Herbert and Lou Henry Hoover were moving into the floor of the Waldorf she took care of, she went to them. She told them she didn't mind if they wanted to fire her, as she was a Democrat and knew she wouldn't fit in. The Hoovers told her that her politics didn't matter, that she seemed like a nice person and was free to stay if she wished. She did.

Daniel Rodriguez had worked as a waiter at the Waldorf since its opening in 1931. He was part of the room service crew that handled the Towers, but was appointed to serve the Hoovers. "Mrs. Hoover honored me by accepting my services right after trying my way of serving," he recalled. From then on, he was only available in his spare time to serve other Tower residents.

After awhile, Daniel asked Herbert Hoover how he should address him. "Daniel," Herbert Hoover said, "you are considered a member of the family and may address me as every member of the family, and they call me 'Chief'." It was a long association. "I served Mr. Hoover continuously, day by day, breakfast, lunch and dinner, for over 25 years, right until a few months before his death," he recalls proudly. "Mr. Hoover dined alone about once a month. He did not show pleasure in dining alone. He was exactly the same toward me when company was there or not. I was the only Mexican, I would say, who has worked for an American ex-President. How could I ever have dreamed of such a thing! It was a very wonderful experience for me."

Because so many friends were often in New York, the Waldorf provided a convenient and lovely setting for continuing the Hoovers' habit of entertaining. They often visited back and forth with friends who lived in New York, too, and both in-town and out-of-town guests remarked that Lou Henry was the perfect hostess at all times.

Even in the Waldorf, Lou Henry demonstrated her familiarity with practical matters pertaining to the home. Edward Anthony, editor of Collier's Weekly and Woman's Home Companion, and his wife, Esther, were fascinated by the first time they had dinner with the Hoovers at the Waldorf. Herbert Hoover greeted them. When Esther Anthony didn't see Lou Henry she asked, "Isn't Mrs. Hoover joining us?" "She will in a minute," Herbert Hoover said. "She's under the table. A light went out, and she knows all about these things, so I let her fix them." Before long, Lou Henry crawled out, slightly disheveled, became formal and said, "How do you do?"

"The Lady" passes on

After she attended a harp concert on the afternoon of January 7, 1944, a sudden heart attack in the Waldorf suite ended the life of Lou Henry Hoover, a lovely lady and Herbert Hoover's companion of 44 years. But, like a choice perfume, the memory of her lingers. After her death, Herbert Hoover took up permanent residence in suite 31-A of the Waldorf Towers and, in time, he resumed having guests, as he and Lou Henry always had.

It is said that the Hoovers' son, Allan, and his wife, Coby, drove down to New York from their home in Greenwich, Connecticut, when they knew Herbert Hoover would be eating alone. Many reports were given of the attention and care they gave him.

Herbert Hoover had a large suite, with two offices, one for the secretaries and, during the 1950s, another for Arthur Kemp, who at the time was his research assistant. He had his own big living room office, where he worked and received guests. He had a bedroom for himself and another for visiting family and guests. There was also a little kitchen, where he could fix snacks.

Fred Farrar, an art director and lecturer on typography and commercial art, described Hebert Hoover's suite as "just beautiful, mint condition, all antique, all genuine, as if it were new. I was told Mrs. Hoover had been interested in that sort of thing and in their various peregrinations around the world they had picked up this stuff." Among the items displayed in the suite was their wonderful collection of Chinese porcelains—the "blue and whites"—that Lou Henry had begun acquiring when she and Herbert Hoover were first married and lived in China. On the walls of Herbert Hoover's office were all sorts of documents of historical interest.

Strolling the streets of New York

"He used to like to walk along Second Avenue and look in the antique shops," Fred Farrar recalls. "John Falter caught him doing that one time and made a quick sketch, and it appeared as a Saturday Evening Post cover. There was Mr. Hoover and his secretary, looking in the window of this antique shop. Falter didn't say that it was Hoover, but it looked like him. So, Hoover wrote to Falter, or mentioned it to someone, and Falter gave him the original."

Ellen Bruback, a secretary, remembers how Herbert Hoover would come into the secretary's office and say, "Let's go take a walk." He'd put on his hat, and they would go down on the elevator and walk up Park Avenue and down Fifth Avenue, stopping to peer into store windows. Herbert Hoover was interested in new buildings under construction. He liked to know what the styles were, what young people were doing, what their activities were and what they were thinking about. In his later years, he couldn't get out as much, but he always wanted to know what was going on.

On the night of March 6, 1961, Herbert Hoover left his suite at the Waldorf for a walk. It was very dark and very late, and, as he came around the corner, he was stopped by a would-be robber. Suddenly,

THE VIEW FROM SUITE 31-A, WALDORF TOWERS
NEW YORK CITY, NEW YORK.

the robber recognized his victim and said, "Mr. Hoover, you should not be walking around in the dark this time of night. Now go home." Herbert Hoover did just that.

Never without a pipe

In talking with Herbert Hoover about pipe smoking, Fred Farrar remembers commenting that "one of the aggravating things about a pipe is that there is never a place around where you can knock it out." The Chief had a solution Fred Farrar admitted he had never thought of. It took an engineer to think of having a stone in a bowl on various tables and desks throughout the suite. He also used the stones for scratching the kitchen matches he used to light his pipe.

Clarence Francis, a friend and a businessman who had spent some time in government, found it interesting that Herbert Hoover never used a pipe more than once without cleaning it. He had about 30 pipes and used to clean them himself. He was very happy when one of the maids, having seen him operate, proved to him that she could clean pipes just as well. Herbert Hoover gloated over the fact that now he had a maid doing that job. After the pipe was cleaned and the bitterness gone, he smoked it again, of course, making it ready for another cleaning.

Herbert Hoover was fondly remembered by Fioravanti Dell'Agnese, who has met almost every prominent person in recent history. Born and educated in Bulgaria, he managed the Waldorf-Astoria Towers and became perhaps the most decorated innkeeper in the world. In discussing Herbert Hoover with journalist Raymond Henle, he said, "He was a very kind man, and he was very approachable...He put you at ease, in other words. With some great men you feel at a distance, but not with Mr. Hoover. It was just like meeting an old friend every time. In the political field we knew when he was upset, though he did not directly discuss it with us. But he might say something, as the French say, 'en passant'—just in passing."

"You know," Raymond Henle replied, "you put your finger on something there, Mr. Dell'Agnese, because I found it very difficult to reconstruct a conversation that I had with Mr. Hoover after I had it, because so much was done with a 'humph' or some little mannerism he had, and it was very difficult sometimes to really form an opinion."

"Exactly, exactly," Fioravanti Dell'Agnese said. "Maybe, though, they speak the loudest."

Radio personality Lowell Thomas, a close friend of Herbert Hoover's, said the person who perhaps knew the most about The Chief's life at the Waldorf Towers was Joe Binns, who for many years was the right-hand-man to Conrad Hilton. When they would walk together along Park Avenue, Conrad Hilton would look across the street and say to Joe Binns, "Some day we must own the Waldorf." With the aid of Joe Binns, he managed to do it, too. Joe Binns felt Herbert Hoover loved the Waldorf and, of course, The Chief had a unique place in the whole official family. Conrad Hilton made Herbert Hoover a member of the Waldorf's board, an honor he seemed to enjoy.

Joe Binns recalls that Herbert Hoover was beloved by everybody at the Waldorf. The Chief had a couple of Irish maids, "who educated their children, some of them becoming university graduates, physicians and lawyers, and they were the old, honest Irish—good-hearted, staunch Catholic kind of immigrants that came to New York in those days. Mr. Hoover used to chuckle when I'd see him and say, 'Well, I made a speech last night, and I saw Nora this morning and she said, "Well, Mr. President, you did pretty well last night, but you made a couple of mistakes,"' and then he would chuckle and say, 'Well, I guess I did all right, because my Irish maid told me I did all right.'"

An end run around Khruschev

When Nikita Khruschev was staying at the Towers, security was tight, and everything was walled off around the Waldorf. Herbert Hoover had to go somewhere, and one of the hotel employees found an Irish policeman and said, "Mr. Hoover wants to get out of here to go some place, but he's not allowed to." The policeman said, "Well, by gosh, if there's anybody in the world can get through this blockade, it's going to be Mr. Hoover, and I'll see that he gets through." And he did.

"I have never known a man with as many devoted friends, the 'do or die' kind who would follow him anywhere no matter how difficult the chore or how little the personal reward," said Allen Campbell, an intimate friend of the Hoover family.

Edward S. Friendly, the television executive, found Herbert Hoover to be a great catalyst for friendships. "I mean any two people, for instance, who had never laid eyes on each other, if we met under the auspices of Mr. Hoover, we became friends."

Many famous people called on Herbert Hoover in 31-A. From that suite he wrote many books, was active in the Boys Club of America and business, and took an interest in world affairs. He had presidents and other prominent people call on him, and he led a well-rounded life with family and friends. He enjoyed attending baseball and football games, watching sports on TV and keeping abreast of the news. The big sadness in his life was the absence of his companion, Lou Henry, during the last 20 years of his life. After being a robust, healthy man most of his life, he suffered some serious illnesses in the last few years before his death at age 90 in 1964.

Few people had occupied as many different dwellings in so many corners of the world as Herbert and Lou Henry Hoover. Samplers have been popular for many years, and an appropriate one for the Hoovers would have been: Home Is Where the Heart Is.

A chronology of addresses
APPENDIX

Herbert Hoover

Aug. 10, 1874-May 1878	West Branch, Iowa	Birthplace cottage
May 1878-Mar. 1879	West Branch, Iowa	unknown
Mar. 1879-Feb. 1884	West Branch, Iowa	2nd house
Summer 1881	Sioux County, Iowa	w/Pennington Minthorn
1882 (8-9 months)	Pawhuska, Oklahoma	w/Laban and Agnes Miles
Feb. 1884-Nov. 1885	Rural West Branch	w/Allen and Millie Hoover
Nov. 1885-Summer 1888	Newberg, Oregon	w/John and Laura Minthorn
Summer 1888-Aug. 1891	Salem, Oregon	w/John and Laura Minthorn
Aug. 1891-May 1895	Stanford University, California	Encina Hall Romero Hall (The Camp)
1895-1896	Western U.S.	Various mining camps
1896	Berkeley, Oakland, California	Working in San Francisco
1896-1899	Western Australia	Kalgoorlie, Coolgardie gold fields

Lou Henry Hoover

Mar. 29, 1874-1876	Waterloo, Iowa	Birthplace
1876-1878	Shell Rock, Iowa	Farmhouse
1878-1884	Waterloo, Iowa	w/brief stay in Texas
1884	Clearwater, Kansas	Brief stay
1884-1890	Whittier, California	w/parents
1890-1899	Monterey, California	w/parents
1890-1898	San Jose Normal School, Stanford University, both in California	Attending college

Herbert and Lou Henry Hoover

Mar. 1899-Sept. 1901	Tientsin, China	Astor House, Racecourse Rd.
Winter 1901-1902	Monterey, California	Cottage built w/Lou Henry's parents
Spring 1902	London, England	"White House" Ashley Drive, Walton on Thames

Fall 1902-Dec. 1907	London	Hyde Park Gate, No. 39 Kensington	Summer 1915	Palo Alto, California	Seward House, 262 Kingsley
Dec. 1907-1917	London	"Red House" Hornton St. W. Kensington	Oct. 1915-1916	Palo Alto, California	Kimball House, 1100 Bryant St.
Summers 1907-1916	Rural England	Cottages at Swanage, Dorsetshire, Stratford on Avon	1917	Washington, D.C.	1628 16th St.
			1917	Washington, D.C.	2221 Mass. Ave.
			1917-1918	Washington, D.C.	1701 Mass. Ave.
Dec. 1908-May 1909	Palo Alto, California	Rented home of Stanford Dean Evelyn Wight	1917-1920	Washington, D.C.	Shoreham Hotel
May 1909-Feb. 1911	New York City	Apartment at 14 E. 60th St.	June 1917-June 1918	Stanford University, California	Gray House, 22 Alvarado Rd.
1911	Stanford University, California		Summers 1917-1918	Chevy Chase, Maryland	"In The Woods" Kensington
July 1912-Sept. 1913	San Francisco	Wheeler House, 1901 Pacific Ave.	Feb. 1918-Oct. 1918	Palo Alto, California	Houston House, 21 Salvatierra St.
Dec. 1913-June 1914	Stanford University, California	Howard House, 12 Dolores St.	1918-1919	Washington, D.C.	1720 Rhode Island Ave.
Sept. 1914-June 1915	Stanford University, California	Hempl House, 355 Cabrillo Rd.	1918-1920	Stanford University, California	Whitaker House, 7 Cabrillo Rd.
1914-1917	New York City	Gotham Hotel	1919	Paris	19 Rue de Lubeck
1915	Washington, D.C.	Willard Hotel			

1920	Palo Alto, California	MacDowell House, 775 Santa Inez
1920	Palo Alto, California	Gregory House, 14 Cabrillo Rd.
1920	Washington, D.C.	1228 17th St. NW
1920	New York City	950 Park Ave.
1920	New York City	993 Park Ave.
1920	New York City	876 Park Ave.
1920	New York City	55 E. 77th St.
June 1920-1934	Stanford University, California	623 Miranda Reservoir Dr. San Juan Hill
1921-1927	Washington, D.C.	2300 S St. NW
Mar. 1929-Mar. 1933	Washington, D.C.	The White House, 1600 Penn. Ave.
1933-1934	Palo Alto, California	623 Miranda
1934-1964	New York City	Waldorf-Astoria Towers